COLOR-CHARGED THROWS

Explode your world with fantastic retro color! Just grab a crochet hook and the boldest, brightest worsted weight yarn you can find, then settle in to create Psychedelic, Sugar Free, Oops My Nails, or any of the seven eye-popping afghans in this collection. Never crocheted before? Not to worry! You'll find these easy crochet projects growing under your own two hands in next-to-no-time. The sooner you get started, the sooner you can lounge on a cool Beach Volley blanket or wrap yourself in a Super Diva throw.

Production Team:
Instructional Editor - Lisa Rickman
Technical Editor - Linda Luder
Editorial Writers - Susan McManus Johnson & Kimberly L. Ross
Lead Graphic Artist - Rachel Burgess
Graphic Artist - Rebecca J. Hester
Photo Stylists - Sondra Daniel & Karen Hall

Oops My Nails

EASY

Finished Size: 49" x 67" (124.5 cm x 170 cm)

MATERIALS

Worsted Weight Yarn: MEDIUM 4

Purple - 25 ounces, 1,375 yards (710 grams, 1,257.5 meters)

Dk Pink - 22 1/2 ounces, 1,240 yards (640 grams, 1,134 meters)

Crochet hook, size I (5.5 mm) **or** size needed for gauge

GAUGE: In pattern,
7 repeats = 6 3/4" (17.25 cm)
and 8 rows = 4" (10 cm)

Gauge Swatch: 4 1/4" (10.75 cm) square
With Purple, ch 15.
Work same as Afghan Body, page 4, for 9 rows.

Each row is worked across length of Afghan Body. When joining yarn and finishing off, leave a 7" (18 cm) length to be worked into fringe.

STITCH GUIDE

CLUSTER (uses next 4 chs)
(Insert hook in **next** ch, YO and pull up a loop) 4 times, YO and draw through all 5 loops on hook.

Continued on page 4.

AFGHAN BODY

With Purple, ch 210.

Row 1 (Right side)**:** Sc in second ch from hook and in next ch, ★ ch 4, skip next 2 chs, sc in next ch; repeat from ★ across; finish off: 71 sc and 69 ch-4 sps.

Note: Loop a short piece of yarn around any stitch to mark Row 1 as **right** side.

Row 2: With **wrong** side facing and working in Back Loops Only ***(Fig. 7, page 24)***, join Purple with sc in first sc ***(see Joining With Sc, page 24)***; work Cluster, ch 4, ★ skip next sc, work Cluster, ch 4; repeat from ★ across to last 2 sc, skip next sc, hdc in last sc; finish off: 69 Clusters and 69 ch-4 sps.

Row 3: With **right** side facing and working in Front Loops Only ***(Fig. 7, page 24)***, join Purple with sc in first hdc; work Cluster, ch 4, ★ skip next Cluster, work Cluster, ch 4; repeat from ★ across to last 2 sts, skip next Cluster, hdc in last sc; finish off.

Row 4: With **wrong** side facing and working in Back Loops Only, join Dk Pink with sc in first hdc; work Cluster, ch 4, ★ skip next Cluster, work Cluster, ch 4; repeat from ★ across to last 2 sts, skip next Cluster, hdc in last sc; finish off.

Row 5: With **right** side facing and working in Front Loops Only, join Dk Pink with sc in first hdc; work Cluster, ch 4, ★ skip next Cluster, work Cluster, ch 4; repeat from ★ across to last 2 sts, skip next Cluster, hdc in last sc; finish off.

Row 6: With **wrong** side facing and working in Back Loops Only, join Purple with sc in first hdc; work Cluster, ch 4, ★ skip next Cluster, work Cluster, ch 4; repeat from ★ across to last 2 sts, skip next Cluster, hdc in last sc; finish off.

Row 7: With **right** side facing and working in Front Loops Only, join Purple with sc in first hdc; work Cluster, ch 4, ★ skip next Cluster, work Cluster, ch 4; repeat from ★ across to last 2 sts, skip next Cluster, hdc in last sc; finish off.

Rows 8-94: Repeat Rows 4-7, 21 times; then repeat Rows 4-6 once **more**.

Row 95: With **right** side facing and working in Front Loops Only, join Purple with sc in first hdc; work Cluster, ch 2, ★ skip next Cluster, work Cluster, ch 2; repeat from ★ across to last 2 sts, skip next Cluster, hdc in last sc; finish off: 69 Clusters and 69 ch-2 sps.

Row 96: With **wrong** side facing and working in **both** loops, join Purple with sc in first hdc; ch 2, ★ skip next 2 chs, sc in next Cluster, ch 2; repeat from ★ across to last 4 sts, skip next 2 chs, sc in last Cluster and in last sc; do **not** finish off: 209 sts.

TRIM

FIRST SIDE

Ch 1, turn; (slip st, ch 2, dc) in first sc, ★ skip next sc and next ch, (slip st, ch 2, dc) in next ch; repeat from ★ across to last 4 sts, skip next sc and next ch, slip st in last 2 sts; finish off.

SECOND SIDE

With **right** side facing and working in chs and in free loops of beginning ch ***(Fig. 8, page 24)***, join Purple with slip st in first ch; (slip st, ch 2, dc) in next ch, ★ skip next 2 chs, (slip st, ch 2, dc) in next ch; repeat from ★ across; finish off.

Holding 4 strands of corresponding color yarn together, each 14" (35.5 cm) long, add additional fringe in end of each color stripe across short edges of Afghan Body ***(Figs. 9a & b, page 24)***.

Beach Volley

EASY

Finished Size: 49" x 63$^1/_2$" (124.5 cm x 161.5 cm)

MATERIALS

MEDIUM 4

Worsted Weight Yarn:
- Variegated - 23 ounces, 1,390 yards (650 grams, 1,271 meters)
- Blue - 19 ounces, 1,150 yards (540 grams, 1,051.5 meters)
- Green - 18 ounces, 1,085 yards (510 grams, 992 meters)

Crochet hook, size H (5 mm) **or** size needed for gauge

GAUGE: In pattern,
(dc, ch 1) 5 times = 3$^1/_4$" (8.25 cm)
and 12 rows = 5$^1/_4$" (13.25 cm)

Gauge Swatch: 5$^1/_2$" (14 cm) square
With Variegated, ch 20.
Work same as Afghan Body, page 7, for 12 rows.

Each row is worked across length of Afghan Body. When joining yarn and finishing off, leave an 8" (20.5 cm) length to be worked into fringe.

STITCH GUIDE

DOUBLE TREBLE CROCHET ***(abbreviated dtr)***
YO 3 times, insert hook in ch indicated, YO and pull up a loop (5 loops on hook), (YO and draw through 2 loops on hook) 4 times ***(Figs. 17a & b, page 25)***.

Continued on page 7.

AFGHAN BODY

With Variegated, ch 198, place marker in fourth ch from hook for st placement.

Row 1 (Right side)**:** Dc in sixth ch from hook, ★ ch 1, skip next ch, dc in next ch; repeat from ★ across; finish off: 97 dc and 97 sps.

Note: Loop a short piece of yarn around any stitch to mark Row 1 as **right** side.

Row 2: With **wrong** side facing, join Blue with sc in first dc ***(see Joining With Sc, page 24)***; ★ dtr in top 2 loops of next ch ***(Fig. 1)***, sc in next dc; repeat from ★ across, dtr in top 2 loops of next ch, sc in next ch; finish off: 98 sc and 97 dtr.

Fig. 1

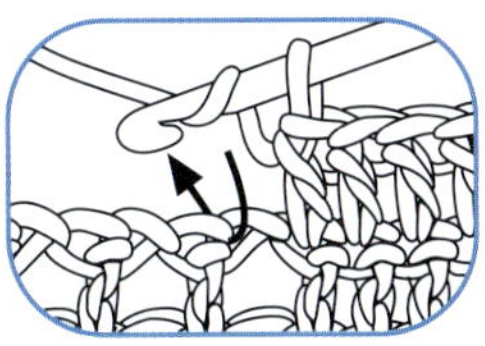

Row 3: With **right** side facing, join Variegated with dc in first sc ***(see Joining With Dc, page 24)***; ★ ch 1, skip next dtr, dc in next sc; repeat from ★ across; finish off: 98 dc and 97 ch-1 sps.

Row 4: With **wrong** side facing, join Green with sc in first dc; (dtr in top 2 loops of next ch, sc in next dc) across; finish off: 98 sc and 97 dtr.

Row 5: With **right** side facing, join Variegated with dc in first sc; ★ ch 1, skip next dtr, dc in next sc; repeat from ★ across; finish off: 98 dc and 97 ch-1 sps.

Row 6: With **wrong** side facing, join Blue with sc in first dc; (dtr in top 2 loops of next ch, sc in next dc) across; finish off: 98 sc and 97 dtr.

Row 7: With **right** side facing, join Variegated with dc in first sc; ★ ch 1, skip next dtr, dc in next sc; repeat from ★ across; finish off: 98 dc and 97 ch-1 sps.

Repeat Rows 4-7 for pattern until Afghan Body measures approximately $48^{1}/_{2}$" (123 cm) from beginning ch, ending by working Row 7.

TRIM

FIRST SIDE

With **right** side facing, join Variegated with slip st in first dc on last row worked; (slip st in next ch-1 sp, ch 1) across to last ch-1 sp, slip st in last ch-1 sp and in last dc; finish off.

SECOND SIDE

With **right** side facing and working in sps and in free loops of beginning ch ***(Fig. 8, page 24)***, join Variegated with slip st in first ch; (slip st in next sp, ch 1) across to last sp, slip st in last sp and in marked ch; finish off.

Holding 2 strands of corresponding color yarn together, each 16" (40.5 cm) long, add additional fringe in each row across short edges of Afghan Body ***(Figs. 9a & b, page 24)***.

Crochet is a cool way to express your creativity or chill out after a stressful day ... and it's fun to do by yourself or with friends. With just a little practice, you'll have a one-of-a-kind afghan that will make your friends green with envy.

Psychedelic

EASY

Finished Size: 48" x 64" (122 cm x 162.5 cm)

MATERIALS

Worsted Weight Yarn: MEDIUM 4

Blue - 21 ounces, 1,155 yards (600 grams, 1,056 meters)

Yellow - 19$^1/_2$ ounces, 1,075 yards (550 grams, 983 meters)

Green - 18$^1/_2$ ounces, 1,020 yards (530 grams, 932.5 meters)

Pink - 18$^1/_2$ ounces, 1,020 yards (530 grams, 932.5 meters)

Crochet hook, size I (5.5 mm) **or** size needed for gauge

GAUGE: In pattern,
(sc, ch 1) 4 times = 2$^1/_2$" (6.25 cm)
and 8 rows = 3" (7.5 cm)

Gauge Swatch: 4" (10 cm) square
With Blue, ch 14.
Work same as Afghan Body, page 10, for 12 rows.

Each row is worked across length of Afghan Body. When joining yarn and finishing off, leave a 7" (18 cm) length to be worked into fringe.

Continued on page 10.

STITCH GUIDE

LONG DOUBLE CROCHET *(abbreviated LDC)*

YO, insert hook in st indicated ***(Fig. 2)***, YO and pull up a loop even with last st made (3 loops on hook), (YO and draw through 2 loops on hook) twice.

Fig. 2

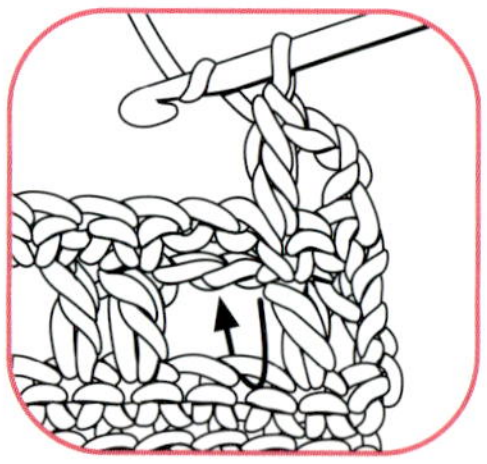

FRONT POST DOUBLE CROCHET *(abbreviated FPdc)*

YO, insert hook from **front** to **back** around post of st indicated ***(Fig. 3)***, YO and pull up a loop (3 loops on hook), (YO and draw through 2 loops on hook) twice. Skip st behind FPdc.

Fig. 3

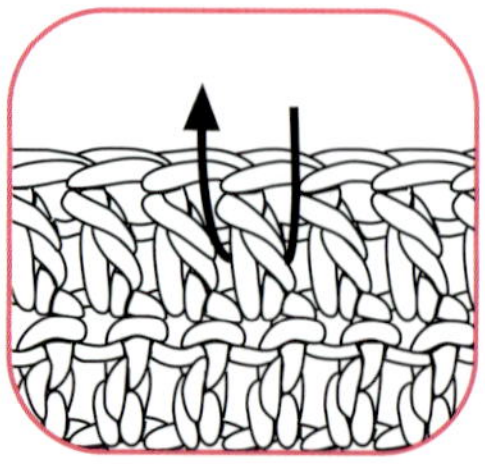

AFGHAN BODY

With Blue, ch 206.

Row 1 (Right side)**:** Sc in second ch from hook, ★ ch 1, skip next ch, sc in next ch; repeat from ★ across; finish off: 103 sc and 102 chs.

Note: Loop a short piece of yarn around any stitch to mark Row 1 as **right** side.

Row 2: With **wrong** side facing, join Blue with sc in first sc *(see Joining With Sc, page 24)*; ★ ch 1, skip next ch, sc in next sc; repeat from ★ across, finish off.

Row 3: With **right** side facing, join Blue with sc in first sc; working in **front** of next ch *(Fig. 6, page 24)*, work LDC in skipped ch one row **below**, ★ ch 1, skip next sc, working in **front** of next ch, work LDC in skipped ch one row **below**; repeat from ★ across to last sc, sc in last sc; finish off: 102 LDC and 101 chs.

Row 4: With **wrong** side facing, join Blue with sc in first sc; ★ sc in next LDC, working **behind** next ch *(Fig. 6, page 24)*, work LDC in skipped sc one row **below**; repeat from ★ across to last 2 sts, sc in last 2 sts; finish off: 104 sc and 101 LDC.

Row 5: With **right** side facing, join Green with sc in first sc; working in **front** of next sc, work FPdc around st one row **below**, ★ ch 1, skip next LDC, working in **front** of next sc, work FPdc around st one row **below**; repeat from ★ across to last sc, sc in last sc; finish off: 102 FPdc and 101 chs.

Row 6: With **wrong** side facing, join Yellow with sc in first sc; ★ sc in next FPdc, working **behind** next ch, work LDC in skipped LDC one row **below**; repeat from ★ across to last 2 sts, sc in last 2 sts; finish off: 104 sc and 101 LDC.

Row 7: With **right** side facing, join Pink with sc in first sc; working in **front** of next sc, work FPdc around FPdc one row **below**, ★ ch 1, skip next LDC, working in **front** of next sc, work FPdc around FPdc one row **below**; repeat from ★ across to last sc, sc in last sc; finish off: 102 FPdc and 101 chs.

Row 8: With **wrong** side facing, join Blue with sc in first sc; ★ sc in next FPdc, working **behind** next ch, work LDC in skipped LDC one row **below**; repeat from ★ across to last 2 sts, sc in last 2 sts; finish off: 104 sc and 101 LDC.

Repeat Rows 5-8 for pattern until Afghan Body measures approximately 47" (119.5 cm) from beginning ch, ending by working Row 8.

Last Row: With **right** side facing, join Blue with sc in first sc; ★ ch 1, skip next sc, sc in next st; repeat from ★ across; finish off: 102 ch-1 sps.

TRIM

FIRST SIDE

With **right** side facing, join Blue with slip st in first sc on Last Row; (slip st in next ch-1 sp, ch 1) across to last ch-1 sp, slip st in last ch-1 sp and in last sc; finish off.

SECOND SIDE

With **right** side facing and working in sps and in free loops of beginning ch *(Fig. 8, page 24)*, join Blue with slip st in first ch; (slip st in next sp, ch 1) across to last sp, slip st in last sp and in next ch; finish off.

For additional fringe, add one 14" (35.5 cm) strand of corresponding color yarn in each row across short edges of Afghan Body *(Figs. 9a & b, page 24)*.

Super Diva

EASY

Finished Size: 49" x 64" (124.5 cm x 162.5 cm)

MATERIALS

Worsted Weight Yarn: MEDIUM 4

Purple - 17 ounces, 935 yards (480 grams, 855 meters)

Dk Pink - 17 ounces, 935 yards (480 grams, 855 meters)

Pink - 17 ounces, 935 yards (480 grams, 855 meters)

Black - 12 ounces, 660 yards (340 grams, 603.5 meters)

Crochet hook, size H (5 mm) **or** size needed for gauge

Yarn needle

GAUGE: In pattern, 5 repeats (20 sts) = 5$^1/_4$" (13.25 cm)

One Strip = 3$^1/_4$"w x 64"h (8.25 cm x 162.5 cm)

Gauge Swatch: 3$^1/_4$"w x 5"h (8.25 cm x 12.75 cm)
With Purple, ch 20.
Work same as Strip A, page 13.

Each row is worked across length of Strip. When joining yarn and finishing off, leave an 8" (20.5 cm) length to be worked into fringe.

STITCH GUIDE

BOBBLE

Ch 4, sc in second ch from hook, 2 dc in next ch, sc in last ch, fold first sc on top of last sc and slip st in skipped ch. Keep Bobble to **right** side.

TREBLE CROCHET *(abbreviated tr)*

YO twice, insert hook in st indicated, YO and pull up a loop (4 loops on hook), (YO and draw through 2 loops on hook) 3 times ***(Figs. 16a & b, page 25)***.

Continued on page 13.

STRIP A (Make 5)

FIRST HALF

With Purple, ch 244.

Row 1 (Right side)**:** Sc in second ch from hook, ch 1, skip next ch, sc in next ch, ★ work Bobble, skip next ch, sc in next ch, ch 1, skip next ch, sc in next ch; repeat from ★ across: 122 sc, 60 Bobbles, and 61 ch-1 sps.

Note: Loop a short piece of yarn around last Bobble made to mark **right** side and bottom edge.

Row 2: Ch 1, turn; sc in first sc, (ch 1, sc in next sc) across: 122 sc and 121 ch-1 sps.

Row 3: Ch 4 **(counts as first dc plus ch 1)**, turn; ★ skip next sc, tr in next sc, ch 1, working **behind** tr just made, tr in skipped sc, ch 1; repeat from ★ across to last sc, dc in last sc: 120 tr and 121 ch-1 sps.

Row 4: Ch 1, turn; sc in first dc, ch 1, (sc in next tr, ch 1) across to last dc, sc in last dc; finish off: 122 sc and 121 ch-1 sps.

Row 5: With **right** side facing, join Black with sc in first sc ***(see Joining With Sc, page 24)***; (ch 1, sc in next sc) across; finish off.

SECOND HALF

Row 1: With **right** side facing and working in free loops of beginning ch ***(Fig. 8, page 24)***, join Purple with dc in first ch ***(see Joining With Dc, page 24)***; ch 1, ★ skip next 3 chs, tr in next ch, ch 1, working in **front** of tr just made, tr in second skipped ch, ch 1; repeat from ★ 59 times **more**, skip next ch, dc in last ch: 120 tr and 121 ch-1 sps.

Row 2: Ch 1, turn; sc in first dc, ch 1, (sc in next tr, ch 1) across to last dc, sc in last dc; finish off: 122 sc and 121 ch-1 sps.

Row 3: With **right** side facing, join Black with sc in first sc; (ch 1, sc in next sc) across; finish off.

STRIP B (Make 5)

Work same as Strip A replacing Purple with Dk Pink.

STRIP C (Make 5)

Work same as Strip A replacing Purple with Pink.

ASSEMBLY

Whipstrip Strips together as follows, placing Strips in the following order: (A, B, C) 5 times.

Place two Strips with **wrong** sides together and bottom edges at the same end. With Black, sew through both pieces once to secure the beginning of the seam, leaving an ample yarn end to weave in later. Working through **both** loops of each stitch on **both** pieces, insert the needle from **front** to **back** through first stitch and pull yarn through ***(Fig. 4)***, ★ insert the needle from **front** to **back** through next stitch on both pieces and pull yarn through; repeat from ★ across long edge.

Join remaining Strips in same manner.

TRIM

FIRST SIDE

With **right** side of long edge facing, join Black with slip st in first sc; (slip st in next ch-1 sp, ch 1) across to last ch-1 sp, slip st in last ch-1 sp and in last sc; finish off.

SECOND SIDE

Work same as First Side across second long edge.

Holding 3 strands of corresponding color yarn together, each 16" (40.5 cm) long, add additional fringe in each row across short edges of Afghan ***(Figs. 9a & b, page 24)***.

Fig. 4

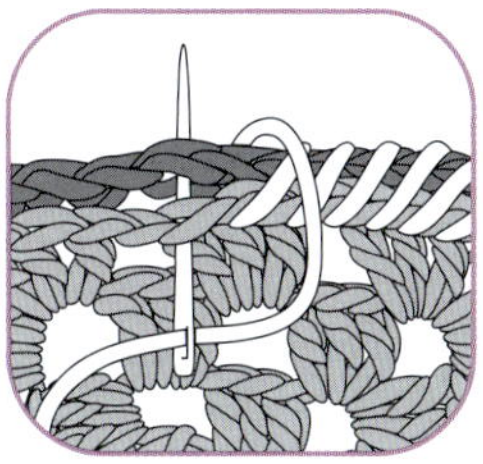

So Fresh

EASY

Finished Size: 46 1/2" x 64" (118 cm x 162.5 cm)

MATERIALS

Worsted Weight Yarn: MEDIUM 4

Orange - 42 ounces, 2,310 yards (1,190 grams, 2,112.5 meters)

Green - 12 1/2 ounces, 690 yards (360 grams, 631 meters)

Yellow - 12 ounces, 660 yards (340 grams, 603.5 meters)

Crochet hook, size I (5.5 mm) **or** size needed for gauge

GAUGE: In pattern,
(sc, ch 1) 5 times = 3" (7.5 cm)
and 12 rows = 3 7/8" (9.75 cm)

Gauge Swatch: 4" (10 cm) square
With Orange, ch 14.
Work same as Afghan Body, page 16, for 12 rows.

Each row is worked across length of Afghan Body. When joining yarn and finishing off, leave a 7" (18 cm) length to be worked into fringe.

STITCH GUIDE

TREBLE CROCHET ***(abbreviated tr)***

YO twice, insert hook in st indicated, YO and pull up a loop (4 loops on hook), (YO and draw through 2 loops on hook) 3 times ***(Figs. 16a & b, page 25)***.

Continued on page 16.

AFGHAN BODY

With Orange, ch 214.

Row 1 (Wrong side)**:** Sc in second ch from hook, ★ ch 1, skip next ch, sc in next ch; repeat from ★ across; finish off: 107 sc and 106 chs.

Note: Loop as short piece of yarn around **back** of any stitch on Row 1 to mark **right** side.

Row 2: With **right** side facing, join Orange with sc in first sc ***(see Joining With Sc, page 24)***; sc in next ch and in each sc and each ch across; finish off: 213 sc.

Row 3: With **right** side facing, join Green with sc in first sc; ★ ch 1, skip next sc, sc in next sc; repeat from ★ across; finish off: 107 sc and 106 chs.

Row 4: With **right** side facing, join Green with sc in first sc; ★ skip next ch and next sc, working in **front** of next ch ***(Fig. 6, page 24)***, tr in sc one row **below**, sc in skipped sc; repeat from ★ across to last 2 sts, sc in last ch and in last sc; finish off: 108 sc and 105 tr.

Row 5: With **right** side facing, join Orange with sc in first sc; ch 1, ★ skip next tr, sc in next sc, ch 1; repeat from ★ across to last 2 sc, skip next sc, sc in last sc; finish off: 107 sc and 106 chs.

Row 6: With **right** side facing, join Orange with sc in first sc; ★ skip next ch and next sc, working in **front** of next ch, tr in st one row **below**, sc in skipped sc; repeat from ★ across to last 2 sts, sc in last ch and in last sc; finish off: 108 sc and 105 tr.

Row 7: With **right** side facing, join Yellow with sc in first sc; ch 1, ★ skip next tr, sc in next sc, ch 1; repeat from ★ across to last 2 sc, skip next sc, sc in last sc; finish off: 107 sc and 106 chs.

Row 8: With **right** side facing, join Yellow with sc in first sc; ★ skip next ch and next sc, working in **front** of next ch, tr in st one row **below**, sc in skipped sc; repeat from ★ across to last 2 sts, sc in last ch and in last sc; finish off: 108 sc and 105 tr.

Row 9: With **right** side facing, join Orange with sc in first sc; ch 1, ★ skip next tr, sc in next sc, ch 1; repeat from ★ across to last 2 sc, skip next sc, sc in last sc; finish off: 107 sc and 106 chs.

Row 10: With **right** side facing, join Orange with sc in first sc; ★ skip next ch and next sc, working in **front** of next ch, tr in st one row **below**, sc in skipped sc; repeat from ★ across to last 2 sts, sc in last ch and in last sc; finish off: 108 sc and 105 tr.

Row 11: With **right** side facing, join Green with sc in first sc; ch 1, ★ skip next tr, sc in next sc, ch 1; repeat from ★ across to last 2 sc, skip next sc, sc in last sc; finish off: 107 sc and 106 chs.

Row 12: With **right** side facing, join Green with sc in first sc; ★ skip next ch and next sc, working in **front** of next ch, tr in st one row **below**, sc in skipped sc; repeat from ★ across to last 2 sts, sc in last ch and in last sc; finish off: 108 sc and 105 tr.

Row 13: With **right** side facing, join Orange with sc in first sc; ch 1, ★ skip next tr, sc in next sc, ch 1; repeat from ★ across to last 2 sc, skip next sc, sc in last sc; finish off: 107 sc and 106 chs.

Row 14: With **right** side facing, join Orange with sc in first sc; ★ skip next ch and next sc, working in **front** of next ch, tr in st one row **below**, sc in skipped sc; repeat from ★ across to last 2 sts, sc in last ch and in last sc; finish off: 108 sc and 105 tr.

Rows 15-18: Repeat Rows 13 and 14 twice.

Rows 19-28: Repeat Rows 7-14 once, then repeat Rows 7 and 8 once **more**.

Rows 29-34: Repeat Rows 13 and 14, 3 times.

Row 35: With **right** side facing, join Green with sc in first sc; ch 1, ★ skip next tr, sc in next sc, ch 1; repeat from ★ across to last 2 sc, skip next sc, sc in last sc; finish off: 107 sc and 106 chs.

Row 36: With **right** side facing, join Green with sc in first sc; ★ skip next ch and next sc, working in **front** of next ch, tr in st one row **below**, sc in skipped sc; repeat from ★ across to last 2 sts, sc in last ch and in last sc; finish off: 108 sc and 105 tr.

Rows 37-140: Repeat Rows 5-36, 3 times; then repeat Rows 5-12 once **more**.

Row 141: With **right** side facing, join Orange with sc in first sc; sc in next tr and in each sc and each tr across; finish off: 213 sc.

Row 142: With **wrong** side facing, join Orange with sc in first sc; ★ ch 1, skip next sc, sc in next sc; repeat from ★ across; finish off: 107 sc and 106 ch-1 sps.

TRIM

FIRST SIDE

With **right** side facing, join Orange with slip st in first sc on Row 142; (slip st in next ch-1 sp, ch 1) across to last ch-1 sp, slip st in last ch-1 sp and in last sc; finish off.

SECOND SIDE

With **right** side facing and working in sps and in free loops of beginning ch ***(Fig. 8, page 24)***, join Orange with slip st in ch at base of first sc; (slip st in next sp, ch 1) across to last sp, slip st in last sp and in last ch; finish off.

Holding 2 strands of corresponding color yarn together, each 14" (35.5 cm) long, add additional fringe in each color stripe across short edges of Afghan Body ***(Figs. 9a & b, page 24)***.

Sugar Free

EASY

Finished Size: $47^{1}/_{2}$" x 64" (120.5 cm x 162.5 cm)

MATERIALS

Worsted Weight Yarn: MEDIUM 4

Blue - 24 ounces, 1,320 yards
(680 grams, 1,207 meters)

Pink - $17^{1}/_{2}$ ounces, 965 yards
(500 grams, 882.5 meters)

Green - 16 ounces, 880 yards
(450 grams, 804.5 meters)

Crochet hook, size I (5.5 mm) **or** size needed for gauge

GAUGE: In pattern,
(sc, ch 1) 7 times = $3^{1}/_{4}$" (8.25 cm)
and 12 rows = $4^{1}/_{4}$" (10.75 cm)

Gauge Swatch: $4^{1}/_{2}$" (11.5 cm) square
With Pink, ch 20.
Work same as Afghan Body, page 19, for 13 rows.

Each row is worked across length of Afghan Body. When joining yarn and finishing off, leave an 8" (20.5 cm) length to be worked into fringe.

STITCH GUIDE

TREBLE CROCHET ***(abbreviated tr)***
YO twice, insert hook in sc indicated, YO and pull up a loop (4 loops on hook), (YO and draw through 2 loops on hook) 3 times ***(Figs. 16a & b, page 25)***.

Continued on page 19.

AFGHAN BODY

With Pink, ch 276.

Row 1 (Wrong side)**:** Sc in second ch from hook, ★ ch 1, skip next ch, sc in next ch; repeat from ★ across; finish off: 138 sc and 137 ch-1 sps.

Note: Loop as short piece of yarn around **back** of any stitch on Row 1 to mark **right** side.

Row 2: With **right** side facing and working in Front Loops Only ***(Fig. 7, page 24)***, join Blue with sc in first sc ***(see Joining With Sc, page 24)***; (ch 1, sc in next sc) across.

Rows 3-5: Ch 1, turn; working in Back Loops Only ***(Fig. 7, page 24)***, sc in first sc, (ch 1, sc in next sc) across.

Finish off.

Row 6: With **right** side facing and working in Back Loops Only, join Green with sc in first sc; (ch 1, sc in next sc) across.

Row 7: Ch 4 **(counts as first dc plus ch 1, now and throughout)**, turn; working in Back Loops Only, ★ skip next sc, tr in next sc, ch 1, working **behind** tr just made, tr in skipped sc, ch 1; repeat from ★ across to last sc, dc in last sc; finish off: 136 tr and 137 ch-1 sps.

Row 8: With **right** side facing and working in Front Loops Only, join Blue with sc in first dc; ch 1, (sc in next tr, ch 1) across to last dc, sc in last dc: 138 sc and 137 ch-1 sps.

Rows 9-11: Ch 1, turn; working in Back Loops Only, sc in first sc, (ch 1, sc in next sc) across.

Finish off.

Row 12: With **right** side facing and working in Back Loops Only, join Pink with sc in first sc; (ch 1, sc in next sc) across.

Row 13: Ch 4, turn; working in Back Loops Only, ★ skip next sc, tr in next sc, ch 1, working **behind** tr just made, tr in skipped sc, ch 1; repeat from ★ across to last sc, dc in last sc; finish off: 136 tr and 137 ch-1 sps.

Row 14: With **right** side facing and working in Front Loops Only, join Blue with sc in first dc; ch 1, (sc in next tr, ch 1) across to last dc, sc in last dc: 138 sc and 137 ch-1 sps.

Rows 15-132: Repeat Rows 3-14, 9 times; then repeat Rows 3-12 once **more**.

Row 133: Ch 1, turn; working in Back Loops Only, sc in first sc, (ch 1, sc in next sc) across; do **not** finish off.

TRIM

FIRST SIDE

Ch 1, turn; slip st in both loops of first sc, (slip st, ch 2, dc) in next ch-1 sp, ★ skip next ch-1 sp, (slip st, ch 2, dc) in next ch-1 sp; repeat from ★ across to last 2 ch-1 sps, skip next ch-1 sp, slip st in last ch-1 sp and in last sc; finish off.

SECOND SIDE

With **right** side facing and working in free loops of beginning ch ***(Fig. 8, page 24)***, join Pink with slip st in ch at base of first sc; (slip st, ch 2, dc) in next ch, ★ skip next 3 chs, (slip st, ch 2, dc) in next ch; repeat from ★ across to last 5 chs, skip next 3 chs, slip st in last 2 chs; finish off.

Holding 3 strands of corresponding color yarn together, each 16" (40.5 cm) long, add additional fringe across short edges of Afghan Body ***(Figs. 9a & b, page 24)***, using photo as a guide for placement.

For a fun "Girls' Night In," throw a crochet party. Invite your friends to bring their latest projects and spend the evening talking or watching a favorite TV show. Don't forget the snacks!

Meeting The Parallels

EASY

Finished Size: 49½" x 68" (125.5 cm x 172.5 cm)

MATERIALS

Worsted Weight Yarn: MEDIUM 4

Black - 39 ounces, 2,145 yards (1,110 grams, 1,961.5 meters)

Blue - 12 ounces, 660 yards (340 grams, 603.5 meters)

Pink - 12 ounces, 660 yards (340 grams, 603.5 meters)

Green - 12 ounces, 660 yards (340 grams, 603.5 meters)

Yellow - 12 ounces, 660 yards (340 grams, 603.5 meters)

Crochet hooks, sizes H (5 mm) and I (5.5 mm) **or** sizes needed for gauge

GAUGE: With larger size hook, in pattern, (sc, ch 1) 5 times = 3" (7.5 cm) and 12 rows = 3¾" (9.5 cm)

Gauge Swatch: 6"w x 4"h (15.25 cm x 10 cm)
With Black and using larger size hook, ch 21.
Work same as Afghan Body, page 22, for 12 rows.

Each row is worked across length of Afghan Body. When joining yarn and finishing off, leave an 8" (20.5 cm) length to be worked into fringe.

STITCH GUIDE

TREBLE CROCHET *(abbreviated tr)*
YO twice, insert hook in ch indicated, YO and pull up a loop (4 loops on hook), (YO and draw through 2 loops on hook) 3 times ***(Figs. 16a & b, page 25)***.

Continued on page 22.

MEETING THE PARALLELS

GIRLS
RULE

AFGHAN BODY

With Black and using larger size hook, ch 227.

Row 1 (Right side)**:** Sc in second ch from hook and in next ch, ★ ch 1, skip next ch, sc in next ch; repeat from ★ across; finish off: 114 sc and 112 chs.

Note: Loop a short piece of yarn around any stitch to mark Row 1 as **right** side.

Row 2: With **wrong** side facing and using larger size hook, join Black with sc in first sc *(see Joining With Sc, page 24)*; ch 1, (sc in next sc, ch 1) across to last 2 sc, sc in last 2 sc; finish off.

Row 3: With **right** side facing and using larger size hook, join Blue with sc in first sc; ★ skip next sc, tr in top 2 loops of next ch *(Fig. 5)*, working **behind** tr just made, sc in skipped sc; repeat from ★ across to last sc, sc in last sc; finish off: 114 sc and 112 tr.

Fig. 5

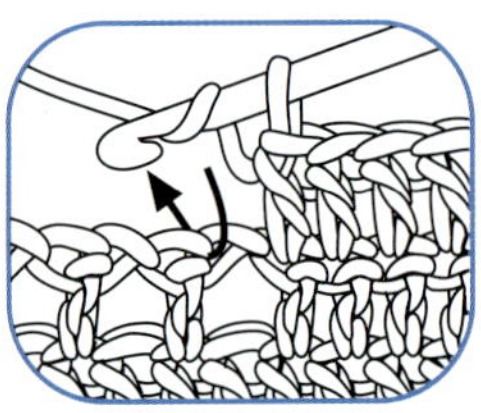

Row 4: With **right** side facing and using larger size hook, join Black with sc in first sc; ★ skip next tr, sc in next sc, ch 1; repeat from ★ across to last sc, sc in last sc; finish off: 114 sc and 112 chs.

Row 5: With **wrong** side facing and using larger size hook, join Black with sc in first sc; ch 1, (sc in next sc, ch 1) across to last 2 sc, sc in last 2 sc; finish off.

Row 6: With **right** side facing and using larger size hook, join Pink with sc in first sc; ★ skip next sc, tr in top 2 loops of next ch, working **behind** tr just made, sc in skipped sc; repeat from ★ across to last sc, sc in last sc; finish off: 114 sc and 112 tr.

Row 7: With **right** side facing and using larger size hook, join Black with sc in first sc; ★ skip next tr, sc in next sc, ch 1; repeat from ★ across to last sc, sc in last sc; finish off: 114 sc and 112 chs.

Row 8: With **wrong** side facing and using larger size hook, join Black with sc in first sc; ch 1, (sc in next sc, ch 1) across to last 2 sc, sc in last 2 sc; finish off.

Row 9: With **right** side facing and using larger size hook, join Green with sc in first sc; ★ skip next sc, tr in top 2 loops of next ch, working **behind** tr just made, sc in skipped sc; repeat from ★ across to last sc, sc in last sc; finish off: 114 sc and 112 tr.

Row 10: With **right** side facing and using larger size hook, join Black with sc in first sc; ★ skip next tr, sc in next sc, ch 1; repeat from ★ across to last sc, sc in last sc; finish off: 114 sc and 112 chs.

Row 11: With **wrong** side facing and using larger size hook, join Black with sc in first sc; ch 1, (sc in next sc, ch 1) across to last 2 sc, sc in last 2 sc; finish off.

Row 12: With **right** side facing and using larger size hook, join Yellow with sc in first sc; ★ skip next sc, tr in top 2 loops of next ch, working **behind** tr just made, sc in skipped sc; repeat from ★ across to last sc, sc in last sc; finish off: 114 sc and 112 tr.

Row 13: With **right** side facing and using larger size hook, join Black with sc in first sc; ★ skip next tr, sc in next sc, ch 1; repeat from ★ across to last sc, sc in last sc; finish off: 114 sc and 112 chs.

Row 14: With **wrong** side facing and using larger size hook, join Black with sc in first sc; ch 1, (sc in next sc, ch 1) across to last 2 sc, sc in last 2 sc; finish off.

Rows 15-158: Repeat Rows 3-14, 12 times.

TRIM

FIRST SIDE

With **right** side facing and using smaller size hook, join Black with slip st in first sc on Row 158; ch 2, (slip st in next ch-1 sp, ch 2) across to last ch-1 sp, slip st in last ch-1 sp and in last sc; finish off.

SECOND SIDE

With **right** side facing, using smaller size hook, and working in sps and in free loops of beginning ch *(Fig. 8, page 24)*, join Black with slip st in first ch; (slip st in next sp, ch 2) across to chs at base of last 2 sc, slip st in next 2 chs; finish off.

Holding 3 strands of corresponding color yarn together, each 16" (40.5 cm) long, add additional fringe in each row across short edges of Afghan Body *(Figs. 9a & b, page 24)*.

A handmade afghan is a great gift for your best friend!

Yarn Information

Oops My Nails
Bernat® So Soft®
Purple - #9850 Lilac
Dk Pink - #75728 Hot Fuchsia

Psychedelic
Bernat® So Soft®
Blue - #75725 Hot Blue
Yellow - #9877 Bright Yellow
Green - #75712 Hot Lime
Pink - #75740 Hot Pink

So Fresh
Bernat® So Soft®
Orange - #75714 Ultra Peach
Green - #75712 Hot Lime
Yellow - #9877 Bright Yellow

Meeting the Parallels
Bernat® So Soft®
Black - #9876 Black
Blue - #75725 Hot Blue
Pink - #75740 Hot Pink
Green - #75712 Hot Lime
Yellow - #9877 Bright Yellow

Beach Volley
Red Heart® Kids®
Variegated - #2940 Beach
Blue - #2850 Turquoise
Green - #2652 Lime

Super Diva
Bernat® So Soft®
Purple - #9869 Purple
Dk Pink - #75725 Hot Fuchsia
Pink - #75740 Hot Pink
Black - #9876 Black

Sugar Free
Bernat® So Soft®
Blue - #75725 Hot Blue
Pink - #75740 Hot Pink
Green - #75712 Hot Lime

Each Afghan in this leaflet was made using Worsted Weight Yarn. Any brand of Worsted Weight Yarn may be used. It is best to refer to the yardage/meters when determining how many balls or skeins to purchase. Remember, to arrive at the finished size, it is the GAUGE/TENSION that is important, not the brand of yarn.

For your convenience, listed above are the specific yarns used to create our photography models.

General Instructions

ABBREVIATIONS

ch(s)	chain(s)
cm	centimeters
dc	double crochet(s)
dtr	double treble crochet(s)
FPdc	Front Post double crochet(s)
hdc	half double crochet(s)
LDC	Long Double Crochet(s)
mm	millimeters
sc	single crochet(s)
sp(s)	space(s)
st(s)	stitch(es)
tr	treble crochet(s)
YO	yarn over

★ — work instructions following ★ as many **more** times as indicated in addition to the first time.

( ) — work enclosed instructions **as many** times as specified by the number immediately following **or** work all enclosed instructions in the stitch or space indicated **or** contains explanatory remarks.

colon (:) — the number(s) given after a colon at the end of a row or round denote(s) the number of stitches or spaces you should have on that row or round.

GAUGE

Exact gauge is **essential** for proper size. Before beginning your Afghan, make the sample swatch given in the individual instructions in the yarn and hook specified. After completing the swatch, measure it, counting your stitches and rows carefully. If your swatch is larger or smaller than specified, **make another, changing hook size to get the correct gauge**. Keep trying until you find the size hook that will give you the specified gauge.

JOINING WITH SC

When instructed to join with sc, begin with a slip knot on hook. Insert hook in stitch or space indicated, YO and pull up a loop, YO and draw through both loops on hook.

JOINING WITH DC

When instructed to join with dc, begin with a slip knot on hook. YO, holding loop on hook, insert hook in stitch or space indicated, YO and pull up a loop (3 loops on hook), (YO and draw through 2 loops on hook) twice.

WORKING IN FRONT OF, AROUND, OR BEHIND A STITCH

Work in stitch or space indicated, inserting hook in direction of arrow *(Fig. 6)*.

BACK OR FRONT LOOP ONLY

Work only in loop(s) indicated by arrow ***(Fig. 7)***.

FREE LOOPS OF A CHAIN

When instructed to work in free loops of a chain, work in loop indicated by arrow ***(Fig. 8)***.

FRINGE

Cut a piece of cardboard 6" (15 cm) wide and 1/2" (12 mm) longer than you want your finished fringe to be. Wind the yarn **loosely** and **evenly** lengthwise around the cardboard until the card is filled, then cut across one end; repeat as needed.

Hold together as many strands as specified in individual instructions; fold in half.

With **wrong** side facing and using a crochet hook, draw the folded end up through a row and pull the loose ends through the folded end ***(Fig. 9a)***; draw the knot up **tightly** ***(Fig. 9b)***. Repeat, spacing as specified in individual instructions.

Lay flat on a hard surface and trim the ends.

Fig. 6

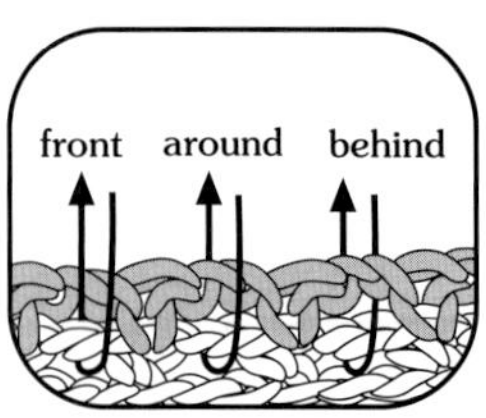

Fig. 7

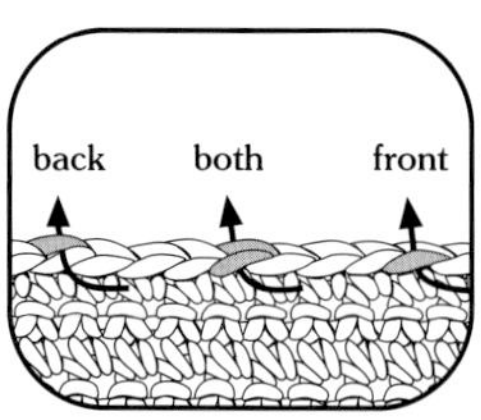

Fig. 8

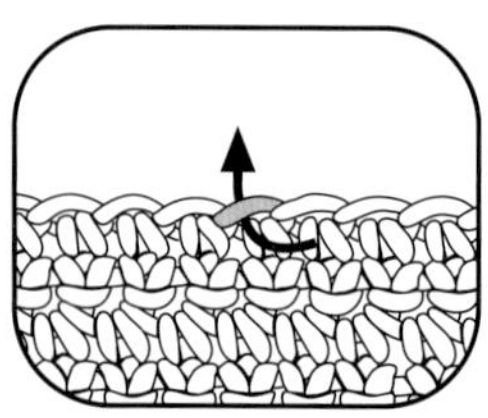

Fig. 9a

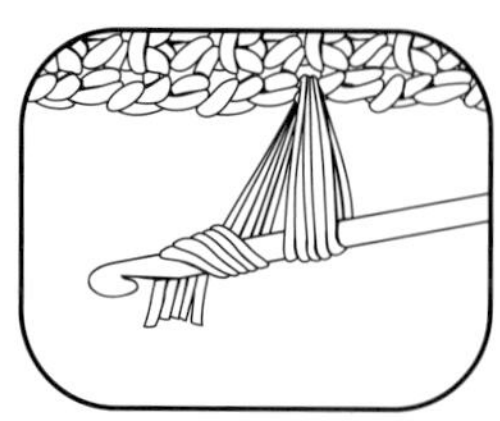

Fig. 9b

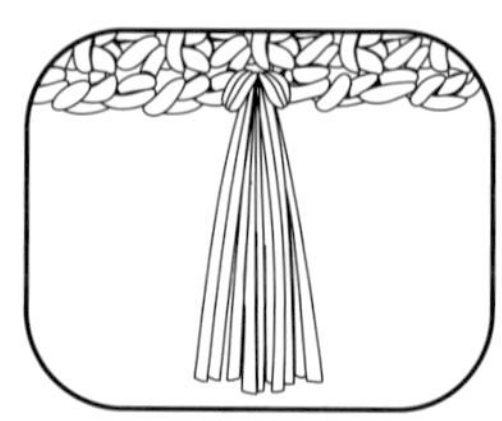

Yarn Weight Symbol & Names	SUPER FINE 1	FINE 2	LIGHT 3	MEDIUM 4	BULKY 5	SUPER BULKY 6
Type of Yarns in Category	Sock, Fingering, Baby	Sport, Baby	DK, Light Worsted	Worsted, Afghan, Aran	Chunky, Craft, Rug	Bulky, Roving

EASY	Projects using yarn with basic stitches, repetitive stitch patterns, simple color changes, and simple shaping and finishing.

ALUMINUM CROCHET HOOKS													
U.S.	B-1	C-2	D-3	E-4	F-5	G-6	H-8	I-9	J-10	K-10½	N	P	Q
Metric - mm	2.25	2.75	3.25	3.5	3.75	4	5	5.5	6	6.5	9	10	15

CROCHET TERMINOLOGY	
UNITED STATES	**INTERNATIONAL**
slip stitch (slip st)	= single crochet (sc)
single crochet (sc)	= double crochet (dc)
half double crochet (hdc)	= half treble crochet (htr)
double crochet (dc)	= treble crochet (tr)
treble crochet (tr)	= double treble crochet (dtr)
double treble crochet (dtr)	= triple treble crochet (ttr)
skip	= miss